HERBERT MURRILL

CARILLON

MUSIC DEPARTMENT

OXFORD
UNIVERSITY PRESS

To Arnold Richardson

CARILLON

HERBERT MURRILL

© Oxford University Press 1949

Printed in Great Britain

OXFORD UNIVERSITY PRESS, MUSIC DEPARTMENT, GREAT CLARENDON STREET, OXFORD OX2 6DP

The Moral Rights of the Composer have been asserted. Photocopying this copyright material is ILLEGAL.

cresc.
ff
[Gt.]
f

* On some instruments it may be found desirable to play this and the similar passage on page 7 an octave higher than written.

f
ff
rit.
a tempo
[Full, without reeds]
[Reeds]
[Reeds off]

Allargando
[Full without Reeds: Sw. closed]
[Reeds]
cresc.
ff
trionfale
[Reeds]
Più allarg al_ _Lento
fff
[Close Swell, and open on final chord. If crescendo pedal is available, play pp ≺ fff]